MONSIGNOR

created by

☆margaret **CARROLL**

☆jerry **McCUE**

art by

☆al **KILGORE**

ABOUT COMICS | CAMARILLO, CALIFORNIA

Monsignor
Originally published by Abbey Books, 1954
About Comics edition published September, 2018

The characters and situations in this work are wholly fictional and
imaginative; do not portray, and are not intended to portray, any actual
persons or parties.

ISBN-13: 978-1-936404-93-3

Customized editions available

Send all queries to *questions@aboutcomics.com*

To

Margaret

"WOW! I WISH WE HAD ONE OF THEM SPACE-
SHIPS RIGHT NOW!"

"OUT OF WORK SINCE LAST XMAS! WHAT CAN YOUR LINE BE, ANYWAY??"

"PROFESSIONAL SANTA CLAUS!"

"OKAY···· BUT NO LIQUID LUNCH!!"

• "DID YOU FIND A BRIEF-CASE WITH SOME PAPERS
   AND BOOKS - - - - - -"
•• "- - - - - AND SOME PEPPERMINT CANDY? YEAH-
   IT'S DOWN AT THE OFFICE WAITIN' TO BE CLAIMED!"

"UM-M-M- MINCE OR PUNKIN!"

"I HOPE THAT GUY WENT TO COMMUNION THIS
MORNING!!"

"- AND THE ANSWER IS **NO** - WE CAN'T AFFORD TO
REPLACE THE DEAD GOLDFISH IN THE SCIENCE ROOM!"
(MEANIE!!)

"YA CAN'T TOUCH HIM IN HERE – CONSECRATED GROUND, YOU KNOW!"

"SEEMS YOU GOT TROUBLES TOO, EH? WELL, LET'S
GO SEE IF WE CAN TALK MRS. O'LEARY OUT OF
SOME CHOW!!"

"IMAGINE-- IF OURS BUTTONED THAT WAY!!"

°"FUNNY THING, OYSTERS ON THE HALF-SHELL
   DON'T AGREE WITH MY UNCLE BIM!"
°°"TELL HIM HE'S NOT SUPPOSED TO EAT THE SHELLS!"

° "I GOT THIS NOTE ASKING ME TO COME HERE – IS IT ABOUT MY BOY?"

°° "RIGHT – THE KID'S BEEN COMPLAININ' – NOW – YOU LAY OFF OF HIS ELECTRIC TRAINS!!"

"PLANT LESS CABBAGE, O'FLAHERTY, MRS. O'LEARY SAYS CORNED BEEF IS SKY-HIGH THESE DAYS!"

"... NO WET PAINT SIGN AND WHAT'S WORSE – YA PAINTED IT ORANGE!!"

"IT'S TIME FOR YOU TO GET A NEW TAXI, MAGUIRE, UNLESS YOU'RE THINKING OF DONATING TO THE SCHOOL FUND!"

"I CAME FOR A DONATION, NOT EXAMINATION, NOW DID YOU HEAR?"

"I HAVEN'T GOT THE NERVE TO TELL HIM TO TAKE
OFF THE POLOROID GLASSES!!"

"POKE TH' COKE, WILL YOU?"

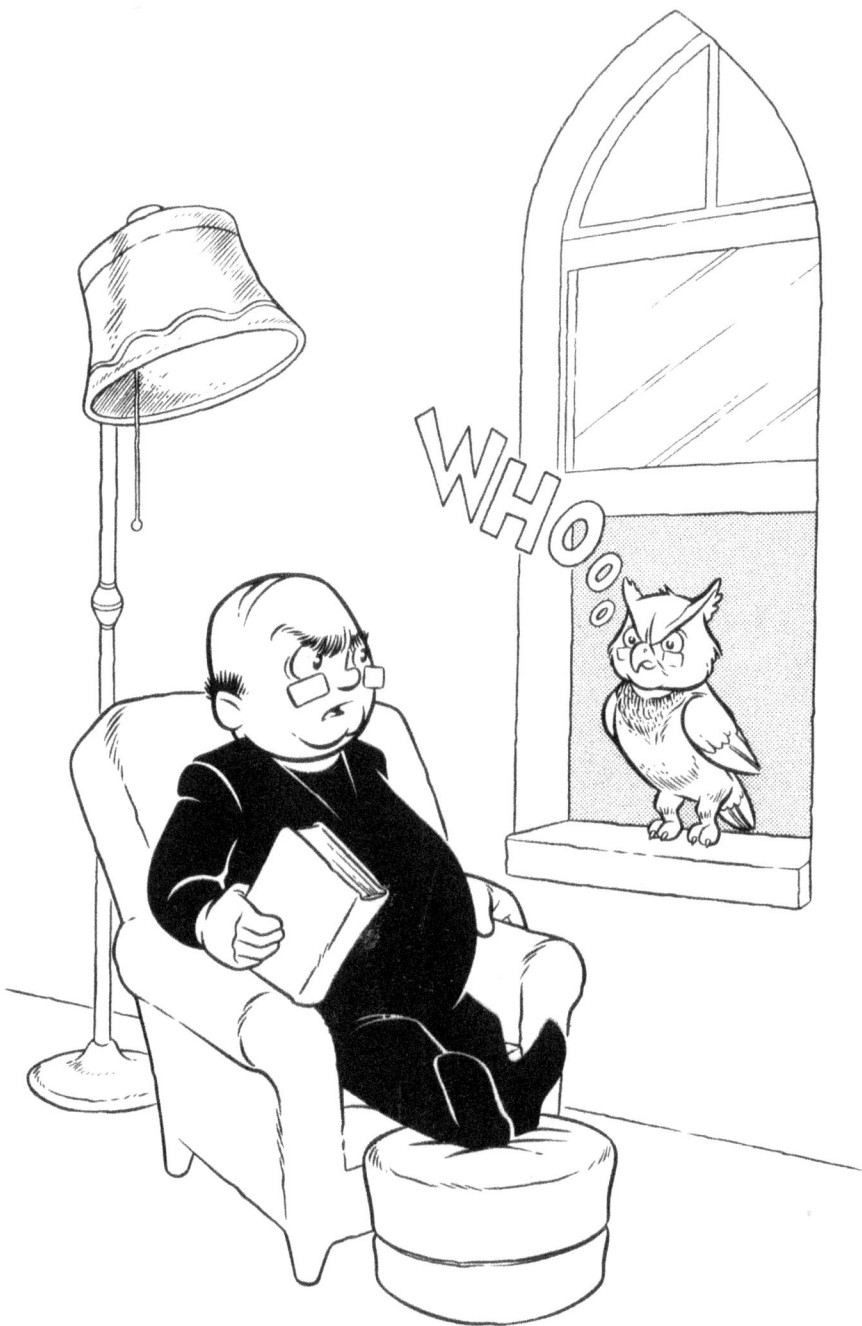

"WELL, WHAT'LL YOU HAVE, MR. WISEGUY?"

"SHAME ON YOU ------ PLAYIN' FIREMAN THIS TIME OF NITE !!"

"MRS. REILLY'S AWAY—BUT YOU'LL FIND THE OLD MAN DOWN THE CELLAR PLAYIN' POKER WITH THE BOYS!!"

"ICE COLD, AIN'T IT?"

"H-M-M – MAYBE A GENIUS, MAYBE A PSYCHOPATH!"

"OKAY, SHORTY- GET IN THERE AND DO YOUR
STUFF!!"

"CURIOUSITY KILLED THE CAT, FATHER!!"

"TELL THE BISHOP I'LL BE DOWN IN A MINUTE!"

"HE'S NOT AS VICIOUS AS ALL THAT --- AFTER ALL,
MONSIGNOR, THIS IS THE FIRST TIME HE'S BIT
A BISHOP!!"

"COME OUTA THERE, O'FLAHERTY AND GET SOME
SNOW SHOVELED—THIS IS NO TIME FOR HIDE N' SEEK!"

"I NEVER KNEW HE WORE THEM, MRS. O'LEARY!"
"I DUNNO, HE SAYS HE'S GETTING SET FER THE ICE CARNIVAL!!"

"— AND THIS IS THE SAME FIGURE EIGHT IN REVERSE
NOW WATCH HOW I FINISH !!"

°"IF IT'S MONSIGNOR YER LOOKIN' FOR, HE'S
  OCCUPIED!!"
°°"NO I AIN'T! ··· AND GET SOMEBODY TO FIX
    THAT CHIMNEY DRAFT!!"

"FORGOT TO TELL YOU, MONSIGNOR, THE BRAKES
ON THIS JEEP DON'T HOLD SO GOOD!!"

"WHY THE INVENTOR HAD TO SCRAMBLE THESE LETTERS LIKE THIS, I'LL NEVER KNOW!"

"HOW DID YOU KNOW THIS WAS CALLAHAN?"
"I RECOGNIZED HIM BY THAT BLOODSHOT EYE!!"

°"YOU KEEP TELLIN' ME WE NEED A CAR FOR OUR EMERGENCY CALLS, OKAY, THERE'S ONE WE CAN AFFORD!"

°°"I'LL SETTLE FOR A BIKE, MONSIGNOR!"

" O, YE SONS OF EVE !!"

"WELL—THERE GOES MY COUGH MEDICINE!!"

"A-A-A-H, SHADDAP!!"

∘"AND TODAY I MADE THIS LUSCIOUS DEEP-DISH
APPLE PIE!"
∘∘"AND TODAY I DESPISE APPLES IN ANY FORM!"

"BUT, MONSIGNOR, WHO'D EVER THINK MURPHY
WOULD BE UP THERE?"

"MAYBE YOU TAUGHT PHYSICS---BUT I THINK
I BETTER CALL THE 'LECTRICIAN, MONSIGNOR!"

"THERE'S NOTHING TO FEAR, WILD ANIMALS ALWAYS RUN WHEN THEY HEAR YOU COMIN'!"

" YEAH, WHICH WAY, MONSIGNOR ??"

"AIN'T HE SUPPOSED TO RUN, MONSIGNOR?"

"THE WORKS, TONY--- BUT BE CAREFUL HOW MUCH YOU TAKE OFF!!"

"- - - JUST MAKE SURE YOU GO TO CONFESSION TOMORROW!"

"HONEST, MONSIGNOR, IT'S WHITE GASOLINE
FER TH' LAWN MOWER!"

"WELL, WHAT ARE **YOU** LAUGHIN' AT? CAN YOU DO ANY BETTER?!!"

"IT WAS A HOT-SHOT OFF THE RIM -- DO YOU THINK THEY'LL SEE IT FROM THE FIRST PEW?"

"BROKE MY GLASSES THIS MORNING --- CAN YOU PLEASE DIRECT ME TO YOUR OPTICAL DEPARTMENT?"

"I DON'T CARE IF HE DOESN'T LIKE FISH ---
TODAY IS FRIDAY!!"

"MIGHT AS WELL CLOSE UP SHOP WHILE HE'S ON!"

(This page reproduced with the permission of
His Excellency Bishop Fulton J. Sheen)

AW- WHY DONTCHA GET IN ON TIME LIKE THE
REST OF US, MICKEY!?"

"LOOKS LIKE JOE, THE BUTCHER, MADE EARLY MASS!"

"YOU MAY HAVE MEANT THAT AS THE WEDDING MARCH – BUT FROM DOWNSTAIRS IT SOUNDED LIKE 'THE SHRIMP BOATS ARE COMIN'!"

"IF YA LET ME IN WITH IT—I'LL KEEP 'EM AWAKE FOR YA!!"

"HEY, O'FLAHERTY, CUT IT DOWN LOW SO I CAN SEE HOME PLATE!!"

"NOW, TELL ME WHY YOU DIDN'T WANT ME TO YANK THIS UNSIGHTLY VINE OFF THE WALL?"
"TOO LATE, MONSIGNOR, IT'S POISON IVY!"

"DON'T WORRY ABOUT IT, MONSIGNOR, THERE'S NOTHING BREAKABLE IN IT!"

"ADIOS, MONSIGNOR!!"

° "I COULDN'T MAKE THE MEETING, MONSIGNOR, BEEN FEELIN' BAD!"

°° "YEAH, FISH-HOOKS IN YER EARS AIN'T GOOD!!"

"HOTTER'N HELICOPTERS, AIN'T IT?"

"WHATEVER IT IS – MAKE ME ONE EXACTLY LIKE IT!"

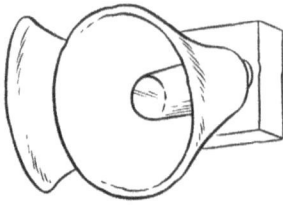

" YOU TELL HIM!!"

"SORRY SIR, SHE'S RIGHT! YOU'RE IN THE WRONG
BERTH, WRONG CAR – AND WHAT'S WORSE - - -
WRONG TRAIN!!"

°"WHAT DO YOU RECOMMEND I DO IN CASE OF
    SEA SICKNESS, DOC?"
°°"THE USUAL THING --- RUN FOR THE RAIL!!"

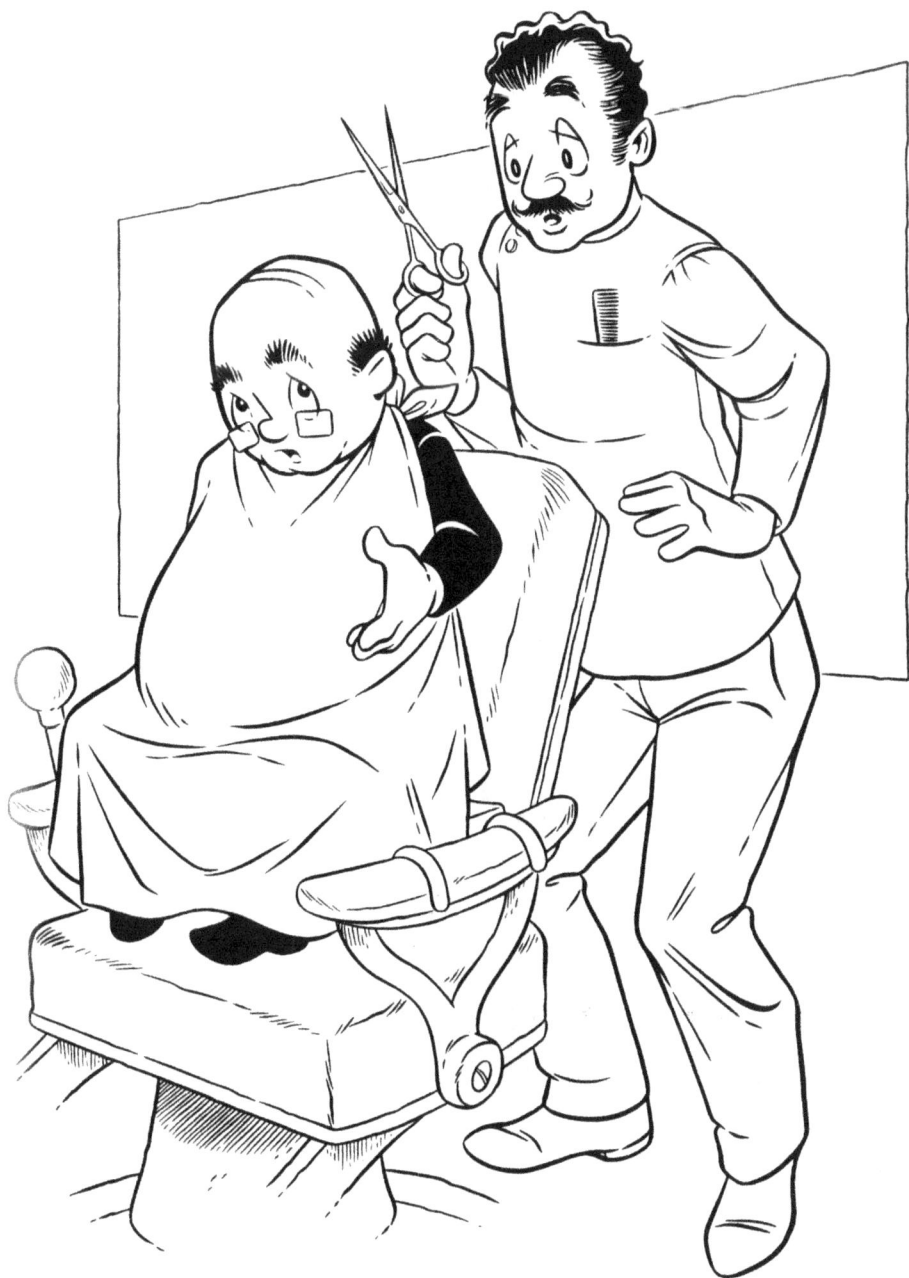

"YEP! TOMORROW I LEAVE FOR ROME—BY THE
WAY, TONY, HOW DO YOU SAY 'CORNED BEEF
AND CABBAGE' IN ITALIAN?"

"*Psst!* Have you seen today's *Daily Nun*??"

Classic Catholic
Cartoon Collections
FROM ABOUT COMICS

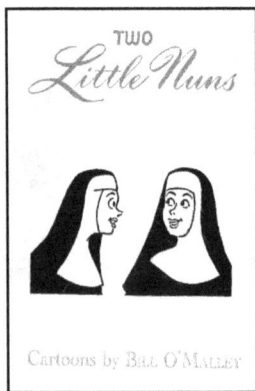

TWO
Little Nuns

Cartoons by BILL O'MALLEY

MORE
Little Nuns

Cartoons by JOE LANE

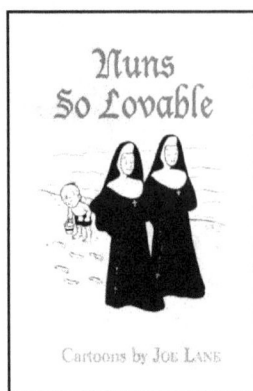

Nuns
So Lovable

Cartoons by JOE LANE

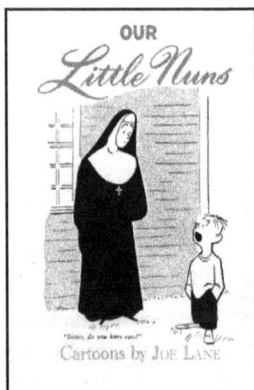

OUR
Little Nuns

Cartoons by JOE LANE

Vale of Dears

Cartoons by JOE LANE

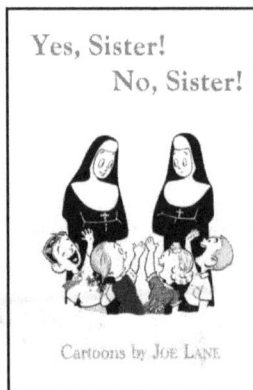

Yes, Sister!
No, Sister!

Cartoons by JOE LANE

Look for them
where you got this book,
or visit *www.AboutComics.com*

Little Gabriel

Al Kilgore